My mind vs Me

by Mar.A

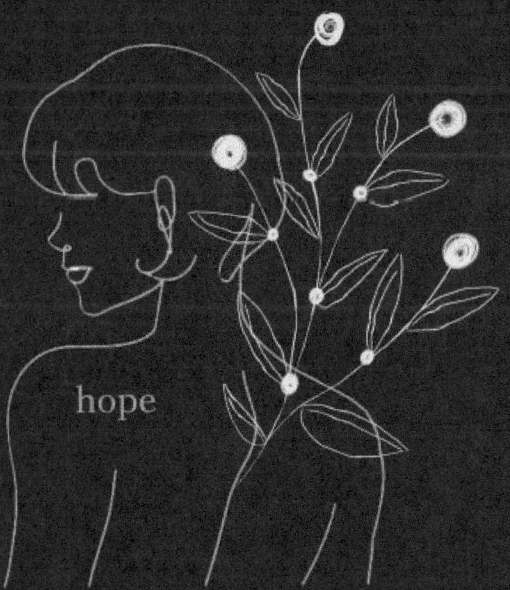

A collection of poetry

Author's note

This book contains some dark content that might trigger some people. So if you are triggered by reading things about depression then please skip the first section of this book or don't read it at all if it makes you uncomfortable.

Any words written in *this font,* are thoughts that run through my mind, put that in my mind while reading so you could have the best experience.

I hope you enjoy it.

Contents

- Losing hope

- hope is reborn

- finding peace

To any soul who has fought
day after day to survive,
this is for you.

My mind vs me

A war has been going on for years.
As a thought fights another and chaos is all I hear.
If you look into my eyes, don't look so deeply, or
you'll see that I'm not as calm as I pretend to be.
My mind gets so loud especially when I'm alone at night.
When everyone's asleep, I'm trying to silence the
demons and make them set me free.
There will never be peace, it will always be
My mind vs me.

Losing hope

I look at the bright sky, it's a sign that maybe
there is hope.
*Remember the last time you thought so you
still ended up alone.*
Years of exhaustion are catching up on me.
I watch as my young always smiling self
slowly disappears, as I still try to figure
out why I'm even here.

I look in the mirror, tears are streaming
down my face.
It's so silent you can't hear a thing, but
only I can hear every single bit of it.
*Why keep going when you know you'll
never win in the end?*

You asked me what was going on with me.
My mouth opened slightly and I almost told
you everything.
*No one will understand, they'll all leave in the
end, taking the piece of you that they broke
with them.*
So I just allowed myself to look at you for
two more seconds then turned my back
and left, before you did so yourself.

I'm tired, I really am.
I take a deep breath as I try to stop my
shaking hands.
I stare at the stars for a little while.
It would be nice to shine like them in
the sky once I'm no longer alive.

You're the reason they all leave.
You're the problem, you have always
been.
Most of the time I try not to listen to
my mind. I try not to believe the voices
because the things they say are just lies.
But this time I know they're right.
You can't hold on to me even if you tried.
Because my shattered pieces will hurt your
hand, and at the end you'll run to save your
life.

Is it that easy for you to hurt a soul
that wanted nothing but to show you
love?
Is it that easy for you to break a heart
that gave you its trust?
Is it that easy for you to forget all the
things I did to see you smile?
Now you just laugh as you watch me
die inside.

I told them my heart was made of glass
and still, they dropped it.
There are too many shattered pieces, I lost
too many of them.
Darling, you're no longer whole, you're
only half human.

You can't force people to choose you.
Trust me I know, but I just want someone
to not walk out of the door.
I want someone who doesn't just love my
smile, but who also loves my flaws.
I want someone who will kiss my scars, and
not run away when life gets dark.

Your words stab like knives.
One pierced my heart and stayed
there for a couple of nights.
Your looks felt like bullets
as they passed through my lungs.

You only said one word
but I didn't eat for months.
And in the end, you still
hated who I have become.

You can't forget the past, you have to
remember, you have to live with it.
I don't want the memories, I just
want to forget.
Every time I close my eyes, I see
someone walking away leaving
me broken behind.
I see myself teary-eyed, waiting for
him to call at midnight.
I see all of their hateful words tearing
me apart like knives.
I see myself getting lost in the dark,
forgetting what it felt like to live
in the light.

You look happy, your eyes are shining bright.
It makes me smile, the look in your eyes.
It almost made me believe that everything will
be alright.
*Do you really believe that one day you'll feel
this warm inside?*

No one picks up a dead flower, they
all just walk all over it.
Just like any rose, I once bloomed too.
Until someone picked me up and put me
in their hair, so they could look good.
But they didn't give me water, and I never
saw the sun.
I couldn't help that my petals slowly started
to fall.
I no longer looked pretty, so they didn't
want me anymore.
They dropped me on the ground like I wasn't
once a beautiful flower just like them all.

I sink my nails into my palms as I watch
you dance with her at the party to the song
that I told you was my favorite.
Because I don't know how to do that.
Forget all about the book once I reach
the ending.
Forget about the characters like they
didn't just completely change me.

I stare at your name on my phone.
He doesn't want you to call.
My heart aches from not hearing
your voice for too long.
I turn off my phone and look at the sky.
I hope you know that I loved you with
every single piece of my broken heart.

Do you think in ten years we'll find
each other again?
Do you think in ten years you'll still love
me the same?
Will you hold on to that magic we
created until we meet again?
*Don't lie to yourself, you know this is
the end.*

Your hold on my hands tightens making
me look at you.
Your eyes are begging me to not let go,
to not leave too soon.
I wonder how you knew, that I was slowly
losing everything, that I was slowly losing
my route.

It might seem like I don't
care.
But I still remember your
birthday and your favorite
cake.
It's just hard for me to show
you love, when I have none
to show myself.

I tried holding on, but my
hand bled and my wrists
hurt.
It was just easier to let go,
when you didn't fight for
me at all.

You're not worth fighting for.

It's too silent inside my mind.
It's driving me crazy that it isn't
loud.
It's like these voices have become
part of who I am.
*Darling, when will you realize that we
are both the same, that we are both
one?*

I can't breathe.
My lungs suddenly feel too small
and I feel so weak.
I can't feel a thing, and it makes me
want to scream.
I want to claw my heart out of my
chest, I want to feel the pain from
all the years.
I can't breathe.
I want to cry, but there are no tears.
I can't breathe.
For the millionth time, I ask myself.
Why am I even here?

I tried so hard, but it didn't make
a difference.
I forgot to sleep, I forgot to eat
just so I could make you proud
of me.
But I saw the sadness in your eyes
when I still wasn't who you wanted
me to be.
I'm so sorry I can't change who I am.
I'm sorry it's that hard to just love me.
You're never enough

I can hear the pain in your cries
like I always hear it in mine.
I want to help but I stay where I am.
Because what will I give you
when I have nothing?
What else can I give you when
you've already taken everything?

Break me, and tear me apart.
I deserve it for not being as perfect
and for having too many flaws.
Open my scars and let them bleed
again.
Use your words to open new wounds.
Just please know that I tried, but I
guess it doesn't matter, right?
You deserve all the pain you feel.

I watch as my blood falls to
the ground.
It looks more black than red,
I think it's tainted from all
the shadows that have haunted
it.

I can feel the guilt burning
through my bones.
All I do is sit there with my
back against the wall.
And I want to get up but it's
just easier to sit back and
watch as everything burns.
I watch as everything I once
was falls like ashes on the floor.
And it feels so empty in my
chest where hope used to burn.
I check my pulse to see if my
heart is still beating at all.

I read the same book a hundred times
expecting the ending to change.
But everything stayed the same.
The places, the characters, and
in the end, she still ends up dead.

I am so lost and I don't know where I am.
I fall to my knees, ignoring the pain that
shoots through me.
I feel so tired; I've been fighting for years.
Please just let me close my eyes and sleep.
*Wake up little girl, there's still a lot you didn't
see.*

My vision of life is getting blurry.
So I close my eyes, the voices in my
mind the only thing keeping me
company.
I clench my hands as it all starts again.
The shaking, the emptiness and the
darkness.
But this time I feel something else.
It's fear.
I'm scared, I don't want the darkness
to take me again.
I don't want to lose myself.
Maybe the fear means you're not really lost
after all, because part of you is still here
waiting for you to find your way home.

If I could talk to my soul I'd apologize.
I would say I'm sorry for hating her
when all she did was keep me alive.
I would say I'm sorry for not understanding
her pain, for being her enemy when she
really needed a friend.
I would say I'm sorry for not believing
that she is more than enough.
You're enough

How did I expect you to love me
when I didn't even love myself?
I guess part of me thought that if
you told me I was special I would
actually, believe it.
But that was unfair and stupid.
Because how did I expect you to
adore my scars when I chose to hide
them rather than drawing hearts
around them?

I can't take my eyes off the moon.
It's shining brighter than usual
tonight, it makes me smile.
And for the first night, there are
no voices keeping me awake and
my heart feels lighter as I close
my eyes.

HOPe IS ReBORN

The moon isn't shining brighter than usual,
it's just that the way you see life has changed.
Because life was never as dark as you imagined
it to be, there's light everywhere.
Follow your heart and it will lead you home again.

Strongly you fought and pieces
of you were lost.
I know you've got too many wounds,
but soon the bleeding will stop
and hope will bloom again.

I am sorry my dear for all that you have seen.
I wish I could erase it, but it will always stay
here.
In the darkest places of your memories, and
in the scars that no one can see.
But trust me this time I will help you heal.

*I know the voices haunted you every day.
I know you hated me for them, but they
only said what you wanted them to say.
I hope the day comes when you see that
I was never your enemy, and I only wanted
to help.*

Open your eyes, you can't hide for long.
You find comfort in the darkness because
it's all you've ever known.
But give the light a chance to dance with
your heart, to show you rainbows, and
to show you love.

The dark times will never leave.
The nightmares will always be here.
But do you want to become one of the
demons or do you want to survive?
As I open my eyes I know that
surviving only won't be enough because
I want to feel alive.

A couple of weeks ago I tried to
picture what my heart looks like.
Darkness was the only thing that
came to mind.
But now I see a little bit of sunlight
on the inside.
And I see some flowers starting to
rise.

You looked me in my eyes and begged
me to let you in.
They'll all leave in the end.
A couple of days ago a thought like this
could've made me rethink everything.
But I'm so very tired of this.
I want to feel it all in every part of
my being.
I don't just want a couple of flowers
in my heart, I want a whole garden.
I want to smile when the birds sing.
I want to wear that sweatshirt just
because you said I looked good in it.
I want to love and to be loved.
I want to feel all the magic.

I made you a bracelet.
I'm not sure you'll like it.
But I guess this is my way
of telling you I tore down
that wall between our hearts
brick by brick.
This is my way of telling you
I'm ready to give you the
remaining pieces of my heart
and the unshattered pieces of
my soul.

~~You're worthless.~~
~~You're not enough.~~
In the same way, there is hell,
there is also heaven.
And while everyone has their
demons, they also have their
angels.
Your demons are so much louder,
they are easier to hear.
But someday I hope you let your
angels reach you when they speak.

The air fills my exhausted lungs.
It feels like they've been starved
for too long.
I feel it as every breath brings back
life to every cell.
It feels as if flowers are growing in
the desert.
It feels like hell is freezing and turning
into heaven.

My nightmares came back last night.
The demons were loud in my mind as
I was fighting to stay alive.
But at the end of the dark tunnel there
was light.
I don't know who saved me this time.

You are the one who saved yourself.
   Can't you see it in the way you're
   fighting for every breath?
   Can't you feel it in your bones?
   Even after everything you still want
   to live.

Every time I climb a mountain and fall
before I can see the view.
I wonder if it's beautiful and if it's worth
all the pain I go through.
Does the sun shine so bright that it blinds
your eyes?
Or does it look like all your dreams finally
became true?

Soon you'll get to see the view too.

I stop myself before I get lost again.
And I mute the voices before they
tell me all the reasons I should hate
myself.
I know this dance all too well.
I cause myself the pain so it doesn't
surprise me when they pull the trigger
and I feel the bullet burn through my
skin.

Show me the world the way
you see it.
Show me the beauty they all
talk about.
Show me the magic in the sunrise
and why you love the dark night sky.
Show me all of it, don't leave me
color-blind.

I was supposed to get the perfect
score and ace this test.
I was supposed to win the first place
and not come in last.
I was supposed to make you proud.
But I painted a picture in my mind of
the disappointment I saw in your eyes.

*It wasn't their disappointment that you
    saw in their eyes, it was yours reflected
    by the light.*

Help me open my heart.
Bring gas and a lighter
and let's burn all of those
bridges down.
Let's break the doors and
remove the curtains.
Help me bring back the
light into my deserted
dark heart.

I want to live something poetic.
Something that makes the sun's
sharp light softens and the stars
to grow brighter.
Something the waves draw back
to look at.
Something as powerful and beautiful
as a supernova.

You didn't feel it but every
cell in your body stared as
a tree grew in your heart.
I think your lungs stopped
breathing for a second
just to savor the moment
when you finally came back
to life.

I still feel the pain from
underneath my scars.
I still hear the demons
in my mind.
But this time there's
something different and
I'm still trying to figure
it out.

I watched as you paved
your way to my heart.
Ignoring all of my
imperfections somehow.
I close my eyes as your
love hits me hard bringing
air to my lungs.
I think I heard the stars
singing somewhere in
the sky.

~~You'll end up alone and broken again.~~

Do you really think that I'm worth it?
What if in the end, I'm the one who does
the hurting?
What if we both end up bleeding?
What if you get haunted by my demons?
Baby, you're perfect and in my mind I
will always be worthless.

"Can I tell you something?" you ask.
I nod slightly.
"I just will never be able to understand
how you can hate anything about yourself.
I look at you and all I see is beauty even
your insecurities and flaws they just
make you shine brighter.
I hope the day comes when you see
the star you really are"
I feel the tear escaping from my eyes.
I am no longer color-blind.

I like the sound of my laugh.
I see the birds standing on
the trees listening to it like
it's music.
Sometimes it cracks a bit
but I guess that just shows
all the things I survived.

~~LAUGH LESS.~~
 LAUGH MORE.
 LAUGH LOUDER.

I'm sorry mum.
I'm sorry for hiding away
in the dark.
I'm sorry if I'm not the
daughter you've always
wished for.
I just wanted you to know
you're the only thing that
kept me going on.

I don't think I'll ever heal.
The pain has forever changed
me.
I can feel it in the way I smile
and how I can't hold my head
high.
But for now, I'm just grateful
that I survived.

Every time I feel myself
going down into the darkest
places no one knows about
I feel your warmth pulling
me in.
Forget about the Earth and the
Sun, I think we created our
own orbit.

I'm still trying to figure out
some things.
Is it okay to cry or is it just
easier to hold the pain in?
Should I always feel alive or
is it okay if I feel a little dead
inside?

You are not supposed to figure it all.
When the clouds are tired they also
let the rain pour.
In Autumn the leaves fall but then
new ones are born.

Why choose me when you can have someone who's perfect?
You might hate your scars but
is it that hard to believe that
someone can love them?
You choose to ask a million
questions when you can let
them go and come to peace
with the fact that you finally
reached the shore.
You don't have to push people
away and you don't have to be
alone.

I don't want you to
feel like you can't
depend on me.
Show me your pain
and tell me about
your nightmares.
I'll be there to listen
and I'll give you my
shoulders.
Hold on to me when
you cry, like the clouds
hold on to the sky.

Dear mind,
I think it's fine if I hurt
from time to time.
You made me hear voices
that made me want to drown.
But you're also the reason
I managed to hear the angels
that somehow kept me alive.
I think it depends on whom I
want to have the mic.
Now I understand that you
suffered too.
You carry my darkest memories.
You've seen me and all of my
dark truths.
We're both hurt and we still
need to heal.
I think it's time to call the war
off because we were never enemies.

peace is reborn

I always do this thing where I
discard everything I have been
through like it's nothing.
But the thing is I have been
through a lot.
It might be nothing for some
people, but for me, it tore me
apart, put me through hell till
I became best friends with the
dark.
It branded me anew.
And it's time that I come to
peace with the fact that I'll
never be the same and that's
okay too.

*You'll still hurt from time to time
and that's all right.
you don't have to become enemies
with the shadows, you just have to
teach them how to dance with the
light.*

I don't feel as guilty when I laugh
anymore.
And surprisingly I don't feel as alone
as before.
It's crazy how I convinced myself that
I had no one at all.
When all these people were waiting for
me to come out from behind my closed
doors.

I'm a fighter, but sometimes a coward.
A lover, who is sometimes scared.
A bright soul that's a little bit tainted.
I'm a human who is so perfectly imperfect.

You played guitar the same
way you played with my heart.
Creating the most beautiful
melodies that were full of
so much love.
You played while I sang the
lyrics.
And together we created the
most special song.

The wind runs through my hair.
The cold numbs my fingers the
same way I used to be numbed
by the pain.
I still have these waves where I
swallow too much water and it
becomes hard to take in the air.
But that's okay because I always
find the shore again.

You don't have to pretend that
life is all smiles and rainbows.
Let the tears fall and let your eyes
create this perfect storm.
Let your heart roar and let it soar.
You don't have to hide your pain
behind some broken doors.

I don't need fixing and I don't
need to change.
If I don't fit in your puzzle that
doesn't mean that I'm bad in
any way.
You're just too blind to see the
light I shine everywhere.

It used to scare me how your
eyes soften when you look
at me.
I didn't want you to pity me.
But now I realize it's not pity
I see.
It's waves of never-ending love
crashing into me.

Let go of the weight on your
back.
Don't hold the rivers back,
they were created to flow.
Swim with the waves and plant
flowers and allow the forests
to grow.

You don't always have to swim
against the waves and the tide.
When tired you could simply float.

For once let the waves do the work
and let them carry you home.
You don't have to bleed to finally
believe that you deserve the
happiness waiting outside your
door.

I smile lightly, the sun setting
my heart on fire.
Or maybe it's just that I saw
your smile.
Let's swim together under the
moonlight.
Darling, you're the reason I
survive.

*The moon witnessed as two souls
intertwined.
They see each other's flaws as
perfections and heal each other's
wounds.
I wish I could write more, but no
words could describe that love.*

I lay on bed, the past replaying
in front of my eyes.
Some memories cause my scars to
tingle and others make me laugh
out loud.
A mixture of pain, nostalgia, and
also some fun.

I miss her.
I miss her carefree smile.
I miss her laugh that used
to make the darkness shine.
I miss the light in her eyes.
I miss me, the one before
the war.

She still lives inside your
heart.
Her eyes shine like a proud
mom.

I was thinking about you.
I'm sure you found your
way in life.
There was a time when your
name brought my demons alive.
But I know now that we weren't
meant to last.
We were just meant to help
each other survive until we
reached the end of the line.

You hold your pen again.
It feels weird, after all,
it's been quite a while.
The words are flowing
everywhere creating
the most beautiful melodies
with your heart.
You feel free, you feel light.
You're so close now to feeling
that peace inside.

If the world ends tomorrow,
I'll spend today talking to the moon.
I'll give my mother one last kiss,
and I'll dance with the stars.
If the world ends tomorrow,
I'll spend the day kissing my scars.
And I'll hold your hand as forever falls
apart.

I wore a dress.
I haven't worn one
in so long.
My hand was itching
for me to put my black
sweater on.
But I turned my back
and went to watch
life in colors.
And I took a picture of the
rainbow.

I couldn't find any words in the
English dictionary to describe
what I have now.
A heart so alive, like a garden
full of flowers.
A mind that is finally at peace,
and that gives me hope every
hour.
A soul that found its home by
looking in the mirror.
The love I have now is so
pure like it has never been
tainted by all the seasons.

I'm dancing in the sunlight.
Shining brighter than the
golden hour.
With every beat of my heart
I become prouder that I
survived, that I'm alive.
And from now on I'll be thankful
for every day that passes by.

I'll sing with the moon,
and dance with the stars.
I'll travel everywhere from
Saturn to Mars.
I'll stand on the sun and not
get burned because my fire
is stronger than any star in
the universe.

I have always believed
that my mind is the enemy.
The voices haunted me,
ruining all the beauty I see.
But the thing is my mind and
me we're the same, we're just
one being.
I only heard what I thought I
deserved to hear, and all the
beauty in the world was ruined
by my fears.
There was no war, it was an illusion
that I created to throw the blame
on anyone but me.
The darkness will always be here
when I'm losing hope, when I am
watching it bloom again and even
when I am finding my peace.
But we can't always drown under
the waves every time one of
our branches break.
We have to survive, thrive, and
do whatever it takes to really live
this life.
We're humans, and that doesn't
make us weak.
Even when you cry, you still shine
brighter than the stars.
And even when you're tired, your
wings can still carry you above all skies.

There will always be peace as long as it's
"my mind and me"

Acknowledgments

Wow, what a ride this was. I wrote this book during some of the hardest times of my life, but also during some of the happiest moments in it. Writing this book has helped me heal some wounds that I didn't even know I had. For me, this was a journey of self-discovery. I poured every part of who I am into this book. By giving you this book, I am giving you a tour of the deepest places in my mind and heart, hoping that this will touch the deepest part of who you are.

This a story through poems. A story about losing every single drop of hope you have but your body still refusing to quit, your soul still fighting to live. This is a story about finally deciding to open your heart again for all the light and beauty in this world. This a story about feeling safe again, about finally finding a version of yourself that you're comfortable in.

I want to thank any soul that read this book from the bottom of my heart. If you felt anything during reading this book, or if this book has helped you in any way then my work here is done.

Thank you to every member of my family. You are the people that give my life meaning. And a very special thanks to my mother. You are my best friend; you are my everything. I can never imagine my life without you. And I can never imagine writing this book if it wasn't for your support.

And finally to anyone who has thrown any kind word my way, to anyone who has believed in me and supported me in any way. I thank you from the bottom of my heart.

Ps: your mind was never your enemy.

Don't miss out!

Visit the website below and you can sign up to receive emails whenever Mar.A publishes a new book. There's no charge and no obligation.

https://books2read.com/r/B-A-WYBW-YCKDC

BOOKS2READ

Connecting independent readers to independent writers.

9 798215 953013